Cross the Finish Line with

ANIMAL CHAMPIONS

Published by Wildlife Education, Ltd.
12233 Thatcher Court, Poway, California 92064
contact us at: **1-800-477-5034**
e-mail us at: **animals@zoobooks.com**
visit us at: **www.zoobooks.com**

ISBN 0-937934-73-9

Animal Champions

Created and Written by
John Bonnett Wexo

Contents

Animal champions are much like human champions—there is something about them that makes them stand out from the rest. Some of them run, swim, or fly faster than other animals. Others can jump higher, dive deeper, or travel farther. A few are champions because they live the longest, grow the tallest, weigh the most, or are simply the strongest.

Animal champions set records just like human athletes do. But it is much harder to measure these records, because they are set in wild places where it is difficult to get accurate measurements. For this reason, most of the records you see in this book are approximate. They are the best guesses that scientists can make.

On these two pages, we show some of the fastest creatures in the animal world. As you read about them, remember that top speed for human runners is 20 to 25 miles per hour. And the fastest human runners can only run at this speed for a few hundred yards.

The honeybee is tiny compared to a human. But it can fly almost as fast as a human can run. It beats its wings an incredible 15,000 times every minute!

Heavy people do not run very fast. But some heavy animals can run with amazing speed. Elephants can charge at 25 miles per hour. And Black Rhinos can run nearly 30 miles per hour, even though they may weigh over 3,500 pounds.

We don't think of ducks as fast creatures. But Canvasback Ducks can fly more than 70 miles per hour when migrating.

Pronghorn Antelope are the fastest land mammals over long distances. They can run at a steady speed of 35 miles per hour for many miles. Their top speed is probably more than 50 miles per hour.

When diving, Peregrine Falcons may reach speeds of *200 miles per hour*. When flying level, Peregrines have been timed at 60 miles per hour.

Hummingbirds move their wings faster than any other birds. Some of them beat their wings 4,500 times per minute.

The Cheetah is the fastest mammal for short distances. It can run faster than 70 miles per hour. But it gets tired quickly and usually stops after a few hundred yards.

For its size, the female House Spider is much faster than a Cheetah. It can run *330 times* the length of its own body in 10 seconds. To match this, a Cheetah would have to run faster than 115 miles per hour.

7

Ostriches can't fly, but they can run faster than any other bird and most other animals as well. They can reach speeds of up to 35 miles per hour and keep it up for 20 miles. They are also the largest of all birds, and they lay the largest eggs.

Size is something we usually judge by our own size. If an animal is bigger than a person, we say it is a big animal. If it is smaller than a person, we say it is a small animal. But we should really judge the size of an animal by *what kind of animal* it is. For instance, a beetle that weighs 3½ ounces may seem very small to us—but it is a giant in the insect world.

Also, when you are talking about size in the animal world, you must remember *what kind of size* you are talking about. For instance, the African Elephant is the *heaviest* land animal in the world. But giraffes are *taller*. Reticulated pythons are *longer*. And, if we count their wingspan, albatrosses are *wider*. In a way, they are all the largest.

More than half of all living mammals are rodents. This group includes rats, mice, squirrels, chipmunks, woodchucks, gophers, porcupines, and beavers. The largest of all rodents is the Capybara of South America, also called the "water hog." These huge relatives of mice can be 4½ feet long and may weigh almost 150 pounds.

The heaviest land animal on record was an African Elephant. It weighed more than 24,000 pounds.

The largest meat-eating land animals are the Polar Bear and the Kodiak Bear. In 1960, a huge Polar Bear was measured after it had been killed by a hunter. It stood *11½ feet tall* and weighed 2,210 pounds.

Goliath Beetles are the heaviest insects on earth. They can weigh more than 3½ ounces— approximately 200 times heavier than a housefly.

Kori Bustards are the heaviest of all birds that can fly. The record weight for a Kori Bustard is 42 pounds.

The title of "tallest land animal" goes to the giraffe. The greatest height ever recorded for a giraffe is 19 feet 3 inches.

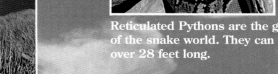

Reticulated Pythons are the giants of the snake world. They can be over 28 feet long.

The Wandering Albatross has the longest wings of any bird. The wingspan for this bird can be as long as 12½ to 13 feet.

Komodo Dragons are the largest of all lizards. They can be 9 feet long and can weigh more than 200 pounds.

Saltwater Crocodiles are the biggest reptiles in the world. The largest ever measured was 25½ feet long and probably weighed over 4,000 pounds.

Humpback Whales are the largest musicians in the world. Male Humpbacks make haunting "music" underwater that can be heard for great distances. It may be that Humpback Whales can actually hear each other when they are more than a thousand miles apart.

*L*ong life is something we usually judge by comparing it to human age. If an animal lives longer than most people do, we say it has a long life. But the oldest human on record lived 122 years, and not many animals can match that. So we don't think that most animals live very long.

But we should really judge the age of an animal according to *the group* that it belongs to, not according to human age. For instance, most insects live less than 1 year, so an insect that lives 50 years is really very old. It lives *50 times longer* than the average insect. If you could live 50 times longer than the average human, you would live to be more than 3,500 years old!

The longest-living fish is probably the Lake Sturgeon. These strange-looking creatures may live to be more than 80 years old.

The oldest bird for which an age can be proved was an Andean Condor (like the one shown above). This bird was hatched in a zoo and lived there for 72 years.

We know that some types of birds can live a very long time. Some people say that a Sulphur-crested Cockatoo (like the one shown at left) lived more than 120 years. But there is no way to prove this claim.

Queen Termites can live and lay eggs for more than 50 years. And some scientists believe that they can live over 100 years.

Gorillas can live a long time, but nobody is sure just how long.
The oldest known Gorilla lived to be 53 years old at the
Philadelphia Zoo.

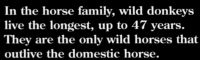

In the horse family, wild donkeys
live the longest, up to 47 years.
They are the only wild horses that
outlive the domestic horse.

Giant tortoises can live
more than 150 years.
Some tortoises living
today were hatched
before the Civil War.

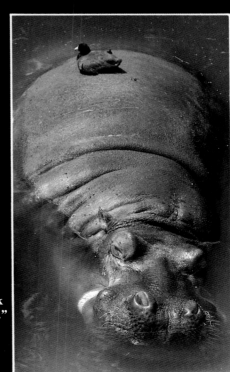

"Hippopotamus" is a Greek
word meaning "river horse."
Of course, hippos aren't
really horses, but they do
live longer than horses—
as long as 50 years.

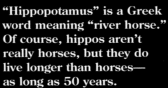

Some species of tree frogs can leap more than *one hundred times* their body length. They "sail" from one tree branch to another, much like a flying squirrel.

Strength and agility are two of the most important qualities for human athletes. Many human champions take pride in their ability to lift great amounts of weight. The strongest human can lift 570 pounds—about two times his own weight. But, as you will see, some animals can do even better than that. For example, there are insects that can lift *50 times* their own weight.

The highest that any human has ever jumped is just over 8 feet. With a pole to help them, some humans can jump as high as 20 feet—more than three times their own height. But there is an insect that can do *66 times* better than that, without using a pole!

When it comes to diving, the deepest that any human has gone is about 285 feet. And the longest that any person has held his breath underwater is about 13¾ minutes. But there is an air-breathing mammal that can dive *37 times* deeper and hold its breath *18 times* longer.

In one hop, a Gray Kangaroo can jump a distance of 44 feet. And when it really gets going, it can leap more than 11 feet off the ground.

Chimpanzees are only about half as tall as humans, but they are three times stronger. They can lift six times their own body weight.

The strongest land animal of all is the Asian Elephant. It can lift more than 2,000 pounds with its trunk. And it can drag a load weighing over 20,000 pounds.

The best divers of all air-breathing animals are the Sperm Whales. These enormous mammals of the sea may dive two miles below the ocean's surface. And while they're underwater, they may hold their breath almost *two hours*!

The tiny Kangaroo Rat is named for its jumping ability. It is actually a better jumper than the Gray Kangaroo. The Gray Kangaroo jumps 8 times the length of its body—but the Kangaroo Rat can jump *48 times* its own length.

Some ants can lift *50 times* their own weight—and they do it with their jaws.

The high-jumping champion of the cat family is the Puma. One of these magnificent cats was seen jumping 18 feet straight up in the air.

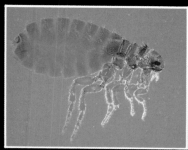

For its size, the Common Flea is the greatest jumper of them all. It can jump *200 times* its own height.

Marathon runners are proud of their ability to run long distances. They run over 26 miles without stopping. But many animals travel much farther. They may go *thousands* of miles in search of food, or to escape bad weather. And some will journey very long distances to find good places to lay eggs or raise their young.

When animals take regular trips like these every year, their movements are called *migrations*. During these migrations they show a determination and endurance that we can only admire. Nothing seems to stand in their way. Many of them cross wide oceans or barren wastelands. Others fly over the highest mountains. Some may swim up the fastest-rushing streams. And they make all of these amazing journeys— across oceans, mountain ranges, and vast wildernesses—without a map to guide them!

The greatest travelers of the mammals are California Gray Whales. Every year, these huge animals migrate *26,000 miles* from feeding grounds to breeding grounds and back again. They swim about 115 miles a day.

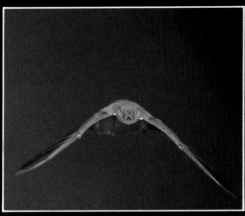

The Red Bat is the champion flyer among the mammals. These bats may migrate more than 5,600 miles each year, and most of that journey is over the ocean.

Siberian Tigers often wander great distances in search of food. One big male walked more than 620 miles in just 22 days.

At the end of their lives, salmon return to the places where they were hatched to lay their eggs. To make this journey, a Chinook Salmon may swim as far as 3,000 miles.

Arctic Terns are probably the greatest travelers among the birds. They may fly *20,000 miles* in a single year—a distance almost equal to a trip around the world.

Caribou often migrate long distances between their winter and summer homes. To get from one home to the other, they may travel 800 miles or more. Along the way, they often have to cross water and other obstacles, but nothing stops them.

Before they can lay their eggs, Green Sea Turtles must return every year to the places where they were hatched. To do this, some of them may swim up to 2,800 miles.

Bar-headed Geese are probably the highest flying birds. They have been seen flying over the top of Mount Everest at an altitude of 29,500 feet—more than *5½ miles up* in the air.

Index